DEVELOPING LITERACY

**Photocopiable
teaching resources
for literacy**

SENTENCE STRUCTURE AND PUNCTUATION

Ages 10–11

Christine Moorcroft

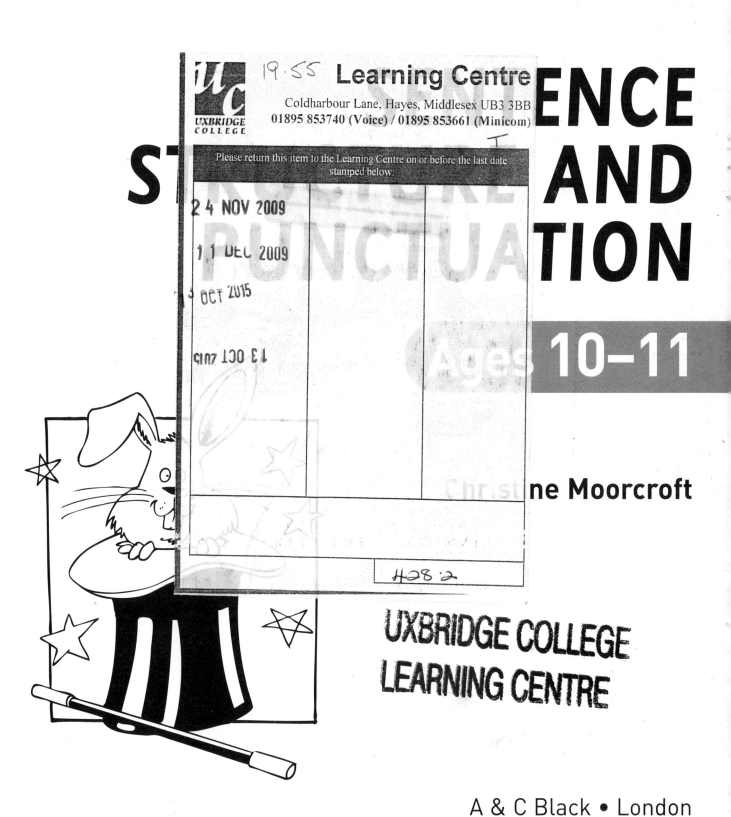
A & C Black • London

Contents

Sentences for biographies, autobiographies, journalism, arguments and persuasion

Poetic sentences

Revision

Published 2007 by A & C Black Publishers Ltd
38 Soho Square, London W1D 3HB
www.acblack.com

ISBN 978-0-7136-8459-9

Copyright text © Christine Moorcroft, 2007
Copyright illustrations © Kevin Hopgood, 2007
Copyright cover illustration © Jan McCafferty, 2007
Editor: Jane Klima
Designed by HL Studios, Oxford

The authors and publishers would like to thank Ray Barker and
Rifat Siddiqui for their advice in producing this series of books.

A CIP catalogue record for this book is available from the
British Library.

Printed and bound in Great Britain by Martins the Printers,
Berwick-on-Tweed

A&C Black uses paper produced with elemental chlorine-free
pulp, harvested from managed sustainable forests.

Introduction

100% New Developing Literacy: Sentence Structure and Punctuation is a series of seven photocopiable activity books for developing children's understanding of sentences and their ability to form sentences.

The books provide learning activities to support strand 11 (Sentence structure and punctuation) of the literacy objectives of the Primary Framework.

The structure of **100% New Developing Literacy: Sentence Structure and Punctuation Ages 10–11** is designed to complement the structure of the Primary Framework for children aged 10 and 11, which focuses on the following types of text:

- Narrative (Fiction genres, Extending narrative, Authors and texts, Short story with flashbacks)
- Non-fiction (Biography and autobiography, Journalistic writing, Argument, Formal impersonal writing)
- Poetry (The power of imagery, Finding a voice).

100% New Developing Literacy: Sentence Structure and Punctuation Ages 10–11 addresses the following objectives from the Primary Framework:

- express subtle distinctions of meaning, including hypothesis, speculation and supposition, by constructing sentences in various ways;
- use punctuation to clarify meaning in complex sentences.

The sentence-level activities provided in this book support the children's reading and writing across different text-types, with a specific emphasis on those listed above: for example, the first section, **Narrative sentences**, focuses mainly on sentences used in fiction. The children learn how to use sentence structure to reveal characters through their own words, through a narrator or through another character's words, how to create an atmosphere and how to convert a story into a play script. They also learn about devices for revealing events which have already taken place, particularly flashback. The second section, **Sentence sense**, supports this by helping the children to understand how sentences are structured (active and passive), how they work, formal and informal language (including official and technical language), standard and non-standard English (including dialect words), older forms of English and how to write sentences involving supposition, hypothesis and speculation. This section also provides a sound foundation for non-fiction writing. **All kinds of words** and **Punctuation** support both narrative and non-fiction writing by focusing on the roles of different words in a sentence and how punctuation clarifies meaning. **Sentences for biographies, autobiographies, journalism, arguments and persuasion** supports non-fiction writing (writing in the first and third person for different purposes, writing sentences to express facts or opinions, discussion sentences and persuasive sentences). It develops the children's awareness of the features of sentences used in different types of writing. The final section, **Poetic sentences**, is linked to the language of poetry, how grammar and punctuation are used effectively in poetry and how words and phrases can be created to communicate meaning and effects.

There is also a section on **Revision**, which consolidates the children's previous learning about grammar and punctuation: it provides activities to remind the children of the functions of different types of words in a sentence, how to use the complete range of punctuation marks to clarify meaning, using tenses and maintaining consistency of tenses, and building complex tenses.

Through the activities the children learn:

- how to adapt sentences to different audiences, purposes and contexts
- how to recognise and write formal and informal sentences, including those used in official and technical language
- about dialogue in prose and play scripts
- about standard English, different types of non-standard English and when they are appropriate, and older English
- about adding clauses and phrases to sentences
- about the effects of word- and phrase-order in a sentence
- about using different punctuation marks
- about the use of auxiliary verbs for forming tenses and about the consistent use of tenses
- about different types of word (for example, adjectives, adverbs, connectives and abstract nouns) and their roles in sentences
- about joining and separating clauses
- about writing sentences to create an effect as well as to communicate information.

Some activities can be carried out with the whole class, some are more suitable for small groups and others are for individual work. They can be used for different purposes: to introduce skills needed for a particular type of writing, to support writing or to help with the assessment of children's progress.

Extension activities

Most of the activity sheets end with a challenge (**Now try this!**) which reinforces and extends the children's learning and provides the teacher with an opportunity for assessment. These more challenging activities might be appropriate for only a few children; it is not expected that the whole class should complete them, although many will be able to do so as a shared guided activity. On some pages there is space for the children to complete the extension activities, but others will require a notebook or a separate sheet of paper.

Accompanying CD-ROM

The enclosed CD-ROM contains electronic versions of all the activity sheets in the book for printing, editing, saving or display on an interactive whiteboard. Our unique browser-based interface makes it easy to select pages and to modify them to suit individual pupils' needs. See page 12 for further details.

Notes on the activities

The notes below expand upon those which are provided at the bottom of the activity pages. They give ideas and suggestions for making the most of the activity sheet, including suggestions for the whole-class introduction, the plenary session or for follow-up work using an adapted version of the activity sheet. To help teachers to select appropriate learning experiences for their pupils, the activities are grouped into sections within each book but the pages need not be presented in the order in which they appear, unless stated otherwise.

The authors and publishers are grateful for permission to reproduce the following:

p.15 extract from *Tom's Midnight Garden* by Philippa Pearce, published by Oxford University Press. Reproduced by permission of Oxford University Press; extract from *Storm Catchers* by Tim Bowler, published by Oxford University Press. Reproduced by permission of Oxford University Press; extract from *The Lion, the Witch and the Wardrobe* by C. S. Lewis, published by HarperCollins. Reproduced by permission of The C. S. Lewis Company Ltd; p.59 extract from 'Cool Medium' from *Absences and Celebrations* by David Sutton, published by Chatto & Windus. Reproduced by permission of The Random House Group Ltd; extract from 'Inexpensive Progress' by John Betjeman, published by John Murray (Publishers) Ltd. Reproduced by permission of John Murray (Publishers) Ltd. Every effort has been made to trace copyright holders and to obtain their permission for use of copyright material. The authors and publishers would be pleased to rectify any error or omission in future editions.

Narrative sentences

The activities in this section focus on the types of sentence used in fiction. The children learn how to use sentence structure to reveal characters through their own words, through a narrator or through another character's words, how to create an atmosphere and how to convert a story into a play script. They also learn about devices for revealing events which have already taken place, particularly flashback. The activities support text-level work on recounts and provide opportunities for the children to select the correct tense and person for the context.

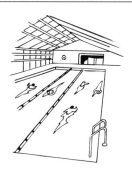

Authors and characters and **Narrating** (pages 13–14) focus on the ways in which authors can use sentences to reveal a character through a narrator, another character or through the character as narrator. They also review previous learning about the consistency of tenses. The children learn to identify characteristics of language: person, pronouns, dialogue and narrative. It is useful to discuss the tenses in the short passages. They are written in the past tense but there is some use of the present tense: for example, in passage 'a' on page 13 and the first passage on page 14. Ask the children why the present tense is used. Draw out that this is not necessarily inconsistent – it helps to establish the time at which the narrator is speaking before a flashback. The present tense is also used in the spoken words in the passage from *The Wind in the Willows* (page 14) since this reports the actual words spoken. Remind the children of this activity when they plan a story. Ask them to decide who is the narrator and how they will introduce the main character.

Scary sentences (page 15) is about sentences which communicate an atmosphere of fear. The feeling of fear is not apparent at the start of each sentence but builds up towards the end or is introduced through contrast. The reader is made to wonder what is going to happen and to expect something frightening. The authors' choices of words help to create this effect: 'an *anxious* tick, tick', 'that *ominous* beat in the air', 'froze in *horror*', '*blood* and *heat* and hair'.

Story to script (page 16) reinforces the children's previous learning about dialogue in narrative and in a play script. It is important to draw out that a play script should tell the actors what to do as well as what to say, and how to say it. The children should first have had opportunities to read play scripts and to notice how they are set out and how the stage directions are incorporated into the script. They could enact the conversation and continue the 'mad tea-party' dialogue with the characters offering one another food and drink, asking and answering questions and making comments about one another and about the setting. They could read the rest of this chapter from the book or online at  http://www.literature.org/authors/carroll-lewis/alices-adventures-in-wonderland/.

Flashback (page 17) reinforces the children's understanding of the past and present tenses and draws attention to the need to maintain the consistency of tenses in a text. They learn about the past perfect (also known as the pluperfect) tense in which the auxiliary verb *had* is used with the past participle (formed with -ed in regular verbs, such as *walked*, *greeted,* and with -en or other ways in irregular verbs, such as *spoken, eaten, gone, thought*). It can be described as 'the past in the past'.

Sentence sense

The activities in this section develop the children's understanding of how sentences are structured (active and passive), how they work, formal and informal language (including official and technical language), standard and non-standard English (including dialect words), older forms of English and how to write sentences involving supposition, hypothesis and speculation. The children also learn how to write complex sentences involving hypothesis, speculation and supposition using conditional verbs and connectives.

Active sentences and **Passive sentences** (pages 18–19) consolidate the children's understanding of the active and passive voices of verbs and how they are used in sentences:

The dog chased the cat. (*The dog* is the agent because it does the chasing. It is also the subject of the verb *chased. The cat* is the object.)

The cat was chased by the dog. (*The dog* is still the agent because it still does the chasing, but it is not the subject of the verb. Instead *the cat* is the subject and *the dog* is the object.)

Draw out that whichever way the sentences are written this does not change the sense of what is said: for example, in the above sentences the chasing is done by the dog and not the cat. It is useful to link this with the investigation of formal language, such as that used in written explanations, and informal language, such as that used in everyday speech and some parts of advertisements. Formal texts usually contain more passive verbs than do informal texts. Discuss why it is useful to know about and be able to use such constructions: for example, active sentences give a direct, immediate feel to the action; passive verbs often have a distancing effect.

Older English (page 20) is about different forms of English. The children learn that English has changed (and that it continues to do so) as new words are introduced, old ones drop out of use and the grammar and structure of sentences change: for example, *pray* meant *please*, we use different names for rooms in houses – bed-chamber (bedroom), scullery (utility room), courtyard (yard) – and instead of saying *I wish*, people used to say *would that*. The structure of questions has changed over the years: from the simple reversal of subject and verb (*Says he so*) to the use of the verb *to do* as an auxiliary (*Does he say so?*). Questions such as *Would it not?* and the tag question *Is it not?* are now more usually expressed as *Wouldn't it?* and *Isn't it?* The children could collect other examples from older novels that they read and try speaking to one another in older English. Link this with work in history.

Standardised (page 21) focuses on the different features of non-standard English: non-agreement of pronouns and verbs or nouns and verbs, double negatives and dialect or slang words. Ask the children to write the meanings of slang or dialect words in brackets, and point out that some of these standard English words give a different meaning, for example *right* meaning *very*. They could also try writing non-standard English versions of leaflets or other non-fiction texts. During the plenary session you could discuss whether it is appropriate to use non-standard English in speech and in writing, and in which contexts. Draw out that the use of standard English ensures that people from other regions understand what is being said or written and that standard English should always be used for formal texts.

All official, **In official terms** and **Impersonally speaking** (pages 22–24) develop the children's awareness of the use of different registers of language for different contexts and consolidate their understanding of active and passive verbs and about the use of the first, second and third persons. They could compare official language with non-standard and dialect English and identify the differences. When changing the sentences on the cards on page 22 to everyday language, point out that, in addition to changing the verbs from active to passive and, in some cases, changing the sentence from the third to the second person, some words need to be changed: *If you are a friend or relation of anyone who works for Whiz Co you are not allowed to enter this competition*; *Please consider other passengers: do not put your feet on the seats*; *If you are under 18 years old you are not allowed to use this equipment*; *If we think you are unsuitable we can ban you/stop you coming in*; *Members – please do not put drinks or spin coins on the snooker tables*; *Please do not dump any type of rubbish on this land*; *Please keep dogs under control at all times, clean up dog waste and put it in one of the bins*; *This area is for people on foot. No vehicles are allowed*; *Please take care – some of the headstones in this cemetery are wobbly*; *We shall list winners of this competition here and write to them*; *Please do not use mobile phones here*; *Please take a ticket and wait for your number to come up.* A class glossary of official terms could be compiled using a table which can order the entries alphabetically. Note that official language is impersonal but not all impersonal language is official: for example, impersonal language is often used when speaking or writing to a large group of people. To support and develop this you could, from time to time, ask the children to listen to you speaking and to press a buzzer or bell, or say 'bleep', every time they hear a non-standard English word or expression. They could collect examples of official and impersonal language from notices, signs and leaflets they find when out and about. Encourage them to bring these into school and to explore other ways of writing the same information or instructions. On page 24 it is helpful initially to encourage the children to respond to the main task without thinking specifically about the technical aspects.

Ask them to think about how the instruction *Children under eleven – bring a grown-up with you* would change if all reference to people were removed or if it were made more official. Getting the feeling of what such language is like, and the kinds of constructions used, will eventually become instinctive. Encouraging this 'working through' and 'sounding out' approach can help. After that, the children should refer to the specific instructions on the checklist as appropriate to help them to formulate their answers.

All in a dialect (page 25) is about the use of words and expressions which are not standard English. Unlike some forms of standard English (non-agreement, incorrect tenses and double negatives), the sentences might be grammatically correct. Dialects have developed in different cultures and in different parts of the British Isles and in other places where English is spoken and in some places (for example, the USA) where different words and different spellings have become standard English. It is important that children are not made to feel that any dialect they use is inferior, but it should be stressed that dialect English is not always appropriate because some people might not understand it: for example, an emergency call was received in Cumbria from a member of the public who reported *sterks* on the beach. The officer who took the call, thinking the person said 'storks', did not think any action was needed because storks would not be in danger or cause a nuisance on a beach. *Sterks*, in local dialect, are cattle. To support and develop this you could, from time to time, ask the children to listen to you speaking and to press a buzzer or bell, or say 'bleep', every time they hear a dialect word. You could adapt this to explore what has become standard English in other countries, such as Australia, South Africa or the USA.

Getting technical (page 26) is about technical language (language related to a specific subject). Here the children consider the language of weather forecasts. They could compare this fairly technical report with those they hear on television or the radio or read in newspapers. Draw out that media reports are written in the sort of language which most people understand, whereas this is written for people who know more about the subject. Help them to collect examples of technical language from handbooks (such as car manuals, cookbooks or dressmaking/knitting patterns). They could look up the technical words and write glossaries to help non-specialists to understand them. Point out that technical vocabulary should be explained or changed to more everyday words unless a text is for people who know the subject. The children could also create glossaries, using a table in Word or other word-processing software. If they create columns for

headwords and definitions, they can instruct the table to sort them in ascending alphabetical order by the first column. This simplifies the addition of new words at a later stage; they can be added to the end of the table after creating a new row at the end of the table by using the Tab key.

Bake a sentence (page 27) develops the children's understanding of how to construct complex sentences through combining simple sentences using connectives and punctuation. Point out, however, that in stories it is not always a good thing to write very long sentences. Sometimes short ones are more effective. Also note that very long sentences are difficult for readers to follow because by the end they might have forgotten what was said at the beginning, and have to reread it. You could display some examples on an interactive whiteboard and invite the children to arrange the sections of the sentences in different ways until they find the most appropriate.

I wonder, **If...** and **Supposing** (pages 28–30) develop skills in constructing complex sentences with subordinate clauses involving speculation, hypothesis and supposition. The children are required to use connectives and conditional verbs. A simple sentence contains one clause. A compound sentence contains more than one clause of equal value, i.e. there are no subordinate clauses. A main clause makes sense on its own as a sentence but a subordinate clause depends on the main clause for its meaning. A complex sentence (also called a multiple sentence) contains at least one main clause and at least one subordinate clause: for example, The girl ate the sandwiches *which her father had prepared for her*. The subordinate clause (italicised) does not make sense as a sentence. Note that a clause always contains a verb. A phrase need not, but can, contain a verb. Sentences that involve speculation, hypothesis or supposition contain a subordinate clause, which is linked to the main clause by a connective such as *if*, *because* or *unless*. The sentence usually contains a verb formed using an auxiliary verb such as *can*, *could*, *might* or *may*.

The sentence improver (page 31) focuses on the structure of a long sentence. The activity will help the children with proofreading and redrafting their own writing. In these sentences the number of verbs can be reduced by combining clauses, through the addition of connectives and by avoiding repetition: for example, *Before she went shopping Sasha asked Paul and Amrit what kind of sandwiches they liked: Paul said ham and Amrit said cheese*; *We think the reason we have never been on holiday is because Mum cannot afford it, although she never admits it, saying that we can find plenty to do close to home – she is right*; *After calling at Jeff's we went to the library, then to the shops and after that to Gran's*.

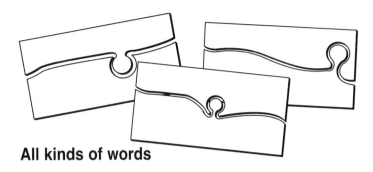

All kinds of words

This section is about the different types of word in a sentence. It consolidates and extends the children's previous learning about nouns, verbs, adjectives, pronouns, adverbs and prepositions. The use of different types of connective for different purposes in several types of text is explored.

Invisible nouns (page 32) develops the children's understanding of abstract nouns. Nouns can be concrete or abstract. Concrete nouns refer to objects which can be touched, heard, seen, tasted or smelled: for example, sand, music, grass, vanilla, perfume. Abstract nouns refer to ideas or concepts: for example, beauty, sadness, royalty. The children will have come across nouns for feelings in Year 5; these could be used as an introduction (possibly linked with work in citizenship). The children could come up with their own ideas for a noun test for abstract nouns: they can have *the* or a possessive pronoun, such as *his* or *her*, in front of them but not usually *a* or *an*, and they do not have plurals. This could be linked with word-level work on adding suffixes -ence, -ance, -ity, -dom, -ism, -y, -ity, -erty, -ness, -th. If appropriate, you could introduce the term *abstract noun*.

Proverbial prepositions (page 33) develops the children's ability to use prepositions as connectives. Whereas conjunctions join units of equal status in a sentence, prepositions show the relationship of a noun or noun phrase to the rest of the sentence. Some words can be used as prepositions or conjunctions: for instance, *before*. Examples of prepositions:

We went out *before* dinner.

She was *ahead* of the others in the race.

There is no smoke *without* fire.

Examples of conjunctions:

We went out *before* the Smiths arrived for dinner.

The weather will be *both* dry *and* cold tomorrow.

She *neither* saw *nor* heard anything.

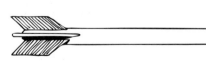

Adverbial arrows (page 34) extends the children's understanding of adverbials (adverb phrases). They learn that adverbs can be phrases which serve the same purpose in a sentence as the adverbs. Emphasise that adverbials give information about a verb by saying how, when, where or why the

action takes place. The phrases on the targets are adverbials, which the children replace with adverbs. (Some high-achieving children might be able to use these terms, but this is not essential; it is more important that they explore the purposes of words and phrases in a sentence.) Discuss the different positions in which you can place the adverb in the sentence:

He *carefully* lifted the baby out of the cot.

He lifted the baby *carefully* out of the cot.

He lifted the baby out of the cot *carefully*.

It's imperative (page 35) focuses on sentences which give instructions or commands using the imperative mood of verbs. It is useful first to remind the children of their previous learning about different types of sentence, their purposes and how to recognise them:

- statement (a declarative sentence, i.e. one which communicates information)
- interrogative (asking a question)
- imperative/command (giving an instruction or requesting action to be taken)
- exclamation (expressing feelings).

The sentences provided on the page are in the form of statements. Example answers: *Take a ticket from the machine and wait for your number to show on the screen*; *Please park in the marked parking bays and not along the roads*; *Switch off the engine before filling the tank with fuel*; *Do not use mobile phones on the forecourt*; *Do not let children use the fuel pumps or air line*; *Please do not make unnecessary noise at night*.

Get connected, **Recount connectives** and **Argument connectives** (pages 36–38) focus on the purposes of connectives in sentences: adding information, a choice, reason or purpose or a condition and linking by time or place. The children develop an awareness of the most useful connectives in recounts and arguments and, in some contexts, of the use of conditional verbs. Explain briefly the benefits of being familiar with and using a range of connectives: for example, being able to control and vary the communication of information rather than using a succession of short sentences.

Punctuation

These activities consolidate the children's understanding of the use of all punctuation marks, including speech marks. They have opportunities to practise their skills in using punctuation to clarify the meaning of a sentence.

Remember the colon (page 39) consolidates the children's understanding of how to use colons for introducing a unit in a sentence. The part which follows the colon explains or amplifies the part which precedes it. A colon can also be used to introduce a list or series or a long quotation. The parts of a sentence which are separated by a colon depend on one another and could not make sense if they were written as separate sentences. You could also write sentences which require colons on strips of paper, give them to groups of children and ask them to cut the strip where the colon should be. They could then glue the strips on to coloured paper and insert the colons in the gaps. Ask them to read the sentences aloud to check them for sense.

Remember the semi-colon (page 40) consolidates the children's understanding of how to use a semi-colon instead of a conjunction for linking clauses. It can also be used for separating long items in a list, especially where the items in the list contain commas. In this activity the focus is on linking clauses. During the plenary session you could ask volunteers to read their sentences from the extension activity aloud while the others listen and say where the semi-colon is. The volunteers could then reread the sentences, inserting a connective word instead of the semi-colon: for example, *My party is at the weekend; it was my birthday yesterday* (*because*).

Commas for separating (page 41) extends the children's understanding of how to use commas to separate clauses, and to surround a clause which adds information to a sentence, in order to make a sentence easier to read and to make the meaning clear. They could read the sentences aloud with a partner and discuss where there should be a slight pause. This will help them to decide where to place the commas. Also try keying in and displaying the sentences on an interactive whiteboard so that the children can try the commas in different places.

Commas for clarity (page 42) develops the children's ability to use punctuation as a powerful tool in expressing meaning. Draw out that by changing the punctuation of a sentence its meaning can be changed – sometimes to give the complete opposite of what is intended. During the plenary session invite volunteers to read the sentences aloud with expression which makes their meaning clear. Discuss how punctuation helps.

Dashes for distance (page 43) extends the children's understanding of how to use the dash as a punctuation mark. It is useful to point out that dashes are not often used in formal writing. They can be replaced by commas or, where two dashes are used to isolate part of a sentence, by brackets. Dashes are more often used, as on this page, in informal writing or quotations. The children could look for dashes in fiction books. Ask them to collect examples for a discussion in which they can explain why these dashes are used. To help, they could write the sentence without the dash and notice the difference.

Bracket It (page 44) develops the children's understanding of when and how to use brackets as punctuation marks in a sentence. They are always used in pairs. For normal punctuation round brackets are used to surround explanatory or supplementary information which would otherwise interrupt the flow of a sentence. The sentence would make sense without the parenthesis (bracketed part), which in some cases could stand alone as a separate sentence but in others might consist of a single word or a phrase.

Sentences for biographies, autobiographies, journalism, arguments and persuasion

This section is about the use of a different person in sentences for different texts. It includes work on person and tense. The use of logical connectives is explored. The children investigate ways of composing sentences for different purposes and to express feelings or create an impression. This is linked to non-fiction reading and writing and helps the children to record and present information in the most appropriate way for the purpose.

This is your life (page 45) focuses on the differences between the language used in biography and autobiography. The children should first have read examples of each and explored the ways in which people's life-stories are presented by themselves and by other people. Here the focus is on the grammar of the sentences in each text-type: biographies are written in the third person, except in quotations and, occasionally, in comments made by the author; autobiographies are written in the first person.

Face the facts (page 46) focuses on the different ways in which facts and opinions are expressed and helps the children to recognise opinions expressed as if they were facts. It introduces some of the verbs which can be used for expressing opinions.

Discussion sentences (page 47) explores the construction of sentences which discuss opposing opinions, with particular reference to connectives for linking these opinions. This could be linked with work in citizenship: the children could listen to discussions recorded in the classroom or from the television or radio and notice the connectives used in any summaries. Also try keying in and displaying the sentences on an interactive whiteboard so that the children can try out different endings.

In a leaflet (page 48) explores ways of writing sentences which engage the interest of readers. The children find ways of enlivening sentences through adding interesting verbs and adjectives: for example, *The walls of the beautiful thirteenth-century abbey*  *rise above the delightful park, with its trees, lawns and colourful flower-beds*; *The lovely old High Street is lined with a variety of shops selling almost anything you might want.* Also try keying in and displaying the sentences on an interactive whiteboard so that the children can try different ways of improving them.

On the web (page 49) focuses on writing headings and summaries in the context of a website home page. If the children could create a website for their group or class to link to the school's website it is important that local authority and school health, safety and security guidelines are followed.

Notes to script (page 50) encourages the children to write sentences based on notes which give the bare facts (but not in complete sentences). They develop skills in filling out notes to form sentences. Discuss how the sentences for a television news report script will differ from those of a newspaper report, and why (they are spoken directly to the audience, who listen to them rather than read them). The children could also write a complete news story developed from the notes or from notes they have made about another issue linked with work in geography or citizenship.

Eyewitness (page 51) is about writing sentences in the present tense about a scene which is taking place, after setting the scene and orientating the audience with a brief recap in the past tense. It encourages the children to consider the purpose of tenses and to use them consistently. Note that using tenses consistently does not mean using only one tense. Discuss how the sentences for a radio news report will differ from those of a newspaper report, and why (they are spoken directly to the audience, who listen to them rather than read them).

Obituary (page 52) is about writing sentences for a report about someone's life, based on notes which are not complete sentences. The children need to consider the appropriate tense, person and language register (formal, informal, personal, impersonal).

Hitting the headlines (page 53) encourages the children to write sentences based on headlines which give the bare facts (but not in complete sentences). This could be used to develop skills in filling out notes to form sentences. To introduce the activity you could cut out news reports and cut off the headlines; ask the children to match the headlines to the reports. This helps the children to recognise the essential points in a text. They could work with a partner to discuss which are the most important points in each report. During the plenary session, compare the results and ask the children to justify why they kept some points but not others. Alternatively, provide reports without their headlines and ask the children to write a headline for each one. This develops skills in identifying the key

facts, summarising a text and writing in a way which appeals to readers. The children could also make up a complete story developed from one of the headlines on this page. Headlines from newspapers could be scanned and displayed on an interactive whiteboard. Invite the children to predict what the story will be about.

Persuasive points (page 54) focuses on the use of persuasive words and phrases. Discuss the effect of these: for example, the use of *we must*, *surely* or *without a doubt* gives the effect that the sentence is communicating a fact and makes the reader feel as if he or she should do something. The children are encouraged to investigate how a text uses language to persuade. This could be linked with speaking and listening and citizenship: some children could prepare a persuasive piece about an issue they think is important to present to the class. The others could listen and ask questions or present challenges.

Argument sentences (page 55) helps the children to write complex sentences which give reasons or explanations to support an argument and to use connectives as a tool.

Poetic sentences

> These activities focus on writing poetic sentences to create images and atmosphere.

A strange image (page 56) encourages the children to explore the power of their choice of adjectives, adverbs and verbs in a sentence in order to create a mysterious effect.

What a surprise! (page 57) encourages the children to explore the use of contrast in sentences in order to surprise the reader. They add an unexpected ending to a sentence.

Word play (page 58) is about playing with words to create humour. It is based on Alice's discussion with the Mock Turtle in *Alice's Adventures in Wonderland* by Lewis Carroll. Examples of word play: boiling/foiling/spoiling, grilling/spilling/thrilling, roasting/boasting/ghosting, stirring/daring/scaring, rolling/strolling, chopping/slopping/hopping, mixing/fixing, simmering/glimmering, icing/pricing/micing, freezing/sneezing, microwaving/micebehaving/micewaving, peeling/feeling/kneeling, weighing/playing.

The issue (page 59) explores how to express feelings about an issue through descriptive sentences and the use of comparison. Before they begin the section on writing their own poem about the effects of text messaging, the children need opportunities to explore this: for example, ask them if they think people speak to one another less if they use text messages – or if they communicate with one another *more*.

Revision

This section provides activities to help the children to consolidate what they have learned about punctuation, tenses and sentence structure. They are reminded about the functions and names of different types of word in a sentence, how to use punctuation marks to clarify meaning, form the different tenses of verbs, maintain consistency of tenses in a sentence or text and build complex sentences through combining clauses and using connective words and phrases.

In a word (page 60) focuses on the different classes of word in a sentence and how to recognise that a word is a noun, verb, adjective or adverb from the other words in the sentence. The children could also use a dictionary to check the meanings of the difficult words used for this purpose and to check their answers. You could also provide sentences in which the same word is used as a noun in one but as a verb in another or as an adjective in one, a noun in another and a verb in another: for example, *There was a stand for holding plants and newspapers, They said I should stand there until told to move*; *There was a set time for dinner, I found a whole set of books, The plaster would set into shape as it dried.*

Punctuation check (page 61) provides an opportunity for the children to use what they have learned about punctuation. The passage requires them to decide where to use full stops, commas, speech marks, apostrophes, brackets, dashes, colons and semi-colons.

Futuristic (page 62) reinforces the children's understanding of tenses, in particular different forms of the future tense. Ask them to read each sentence silently, adding each version of the future tense in turn, before they decide which is the most appropriate.

Past problem (page 63) reinforces the children's understanding of tenses, in particular different forms of the past tense including the conditional past tense. Ask them to read each sentence silently, adding each version of the past tense in turn, before they decide which is the most appropriate.

Sentence-builder (page 64) is about linking four pieces of information in one sentence. It requires the children to consider connectives and punctuation. Encourage them to try different ways of doing this on scrap paper before they decide which is the best.

Using the CD-ROM

The PC CD-ROM included with this book contains an easy-to-use software program that allows you to print out pages from the book, to view them (e.g. on an interactive whiteboard) or to customise the activities to suit the needs of your pupils.

Getting started

It's easy to run the software. Simply insert the CD-ROM into your CD drive and the disk should autorun and launch the interface in your web browser.

If the disk does not autorun, open 'My Computer' and select the CD drive, then open the file 'start.html'.

Please note: this CD-ROM is designed for use on a PC. It will also run on most Apple Macintosh computers in Safari however, due to the differences between Mac and PC fonts, you may experience some unavoidable variations in the typography and page layouts of the activity sheets.

The Menu screen

Four options are available to you from the main menu screen.

The first option takes you to the Activity Sheets screen, where you can choose an activity sheet to edit or print out using Microsoft Word.

(If you do not have the Microsoft Office suite, you might like to consider using OpenOffice instead. This is a multi-platform and multi-lingual office suite, and an 'open-source' project. It is compatible with all other major office suites, and the product is free to download, use and distribute. The homepage for OpenOffice on the Internet is: www.openoffice.org.)

The second option on the main menu screen opens a PDF file of the entire book using Adobe Reader (see below). This format is ideal for printing out copies of the activity sheets or for displaying them, for example on an interactive whiteboard.

The third option allows you to choose a page to edit from a text-only list of the activity sheets, as an alternative to the graphical interface on the Activity Sheets screen.

Adobe Reader is free to download and to use. If it is not already installed on your computer, the fourth link takes you to the download page on the Adobe website.

You can also navigate directly to any of the three screens at any time by using the tabs at the top.

The Activity Sheets screen

This screen shows thumbnails of all the activity sheets in the book. Rolling the mouse over a thumbnail highlights the page number and also brings up a preview image of the page.

Click on the thumbnail to open a version of the page in Microsoft Word (or an equivalent software program, see above.) The full range of editing tools are available to you here to customise the page to suit the needs of your particular pupils. You can print out copies of the page or save a copy of your edited version onto your computer.

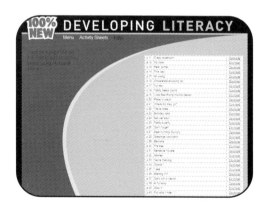

The Index screen

This is a text-only version of the Activity Sheets screen described above. Choose an activity sheet and click on the 'download' link to open a version of the page in Microsoft Word to edit or print out.

Technical support

If you have any questions regarding the *100% New Developing Literacy* or *Developing Mathematics* software, please email us at the address below. We will get back to you as quickly as possible.

educationalsales@acblack.com

Authors and characters

Is the [narrator] the author or a character?

Think about person, names and pronouns.

- **Explain how you can tell.**

a To this day Jane and Michael cannot be sure of what happened then. All they know for certain is that, as soon as Mr. Wigg had appealed to Mary Poppins, the table began to wriggle on its legs.

Mary Poppins by P. L. Travers

b We walked on for about four hours or more, till we came to a little tongue of land which ran out into the sea, and on which was a hill from whose top we might have a wide view.

The Swiss Family Robinson by Johann Wyss

c I tossed a coin – heads right, tails left – and it fell heads, so I turned to the north.

The Thirty-Nine Steps by John Buchan

d Farmer Broadbent hired little Harry Twiggs, who was one of the poorest boys in the parish, at threepence a day, to frighten away the birds.

Little Harry Twiggs' Picnic by Mary Howitt

e Then away out in the woods I heard the kind of sound that a ghost makes when it wants to tell about something that's on its mind.

The Adventures of Huckleberry Finn by Mark Twain

f He was afraid for the minute but it is impossible for a mongoose to stay frightened for any length of time, and though Rikki-tikki had never met a live cobra before, his mother had fed him on dead ones.

The Jungle Book by Rudyard Kipling

Sentence	Narrator	How I can tell
a		
b		
c		
d		
e		
f		

NOW TRY THIS!

- **Choose three sentences from above.**
- **Rewrite each sentence from the point of view of a different narrator.**

Teachers' note Introduce or remind the children of the term *narrator* and use fiction books the children know to help them to identify the narrator: the author, the main character or another character. Discuss how to tell, including the use of the first or third person.

100% New Developing Literacy Sentence Structure and Punctuation: Ages 10–11 © A & C BLACK

Who tells the reader about the | main character | **in these sentences from stories?**

- **Write in the boxes:**

| the author as narrator | main character | another character |

My name is John Trenchard, and I was fifteen years of age when this story begins.

Moonfleet by John Meade Falkner

Once upon a time there was a little chimney-sweep and his name was Tom.

The Water Babies by Charles Kingsley

When Mary Lennox was sent to Misselthwaite Manor to live with her uncle everybody said she was the most disagreeable-looking child ever seen.

The Secret Garden by Frances Hodgson Burnett

Charles Simms was always mean, and that's the truth of it. Thing is we never knew just how mean he was until a year back when all the wells in our part of Mississippi went dry.

The Well by Mildred D. Taylor

To begin my life with the beginning, I record that I was born (as I have been informed and believe) on a Friday, at twelve o'clock at night. It was remarked that the clock began to strike, and I began to cry, simultaneously.

David Copperfield by Charles Dickens

'He is indeed the best of animals,' replied Rat. 'So simple, so good-natured, and so affectionate. Perhaps he's not very clever – we can't all be geniuses; and it may be that he is both boastful and conceited. But he has got some great qualities, has Toady.'

The Wind in the Willows by Kenneth Grahame

NOW TRY THIS!

- **Explain how the authors above tell the reader about the main character.**

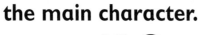 Narrative?  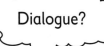 Dialogue?

Teachers' note Before the children complete this page, use the passages on page 13 to show how an author introduces a character: through the author's narrative, through the words of another character or through the words of the character himself or herself.

100% New Developing Literacy Sentence Structure and Punctuation: Ages 10-11 © A & C BLACK

Scary sentences

How does each sentence give a feeling of fear?

What effect do the words and punctuation have?

- Write your answers on the chart.

a 'Hurry,' whispered the house and the grandfather clock at the heart of it beat an anxious tick, tick.
Tom's Midnight Garden by Philippa Pearce

b It was now about seven o'clock, and as I waited I heard once again that ominous beat in the air.
The Thirty-Nine Steps by John Buchan

c She chuckled and reached out to close the curtain; then froze in horror.
Storm Catchers by Tim Bowler

d He was tugging and pulling and the Wolf seemed neither alive nor dead, and its bared teeth knocked against his forehead, and everything was blood and heat and hair.
The Lion, the Witch and the Wardrobe by C. S. Lewis

Sentence	How punctuation affects the sentence	Choice of words. Give examples.		
		Nouns	**Verbs**	**Adjectives**
a				
b				
c				
d				

NOW TRY THIS!

- Write three different sentences that create fear.

Teachers' note Read sentence 'a' with the children and ask them how it makes them feel. Draw out that the imagery of the heartbeat helps to create suspense and to make the reader want the character to hurry. Focus on the expressive verbs *whispered* and *beat* and the powerful adjective *anxious*. Stress that the children may not need to write a word in every box.

100% New Developing Literacy Sentence Structure and Punctuation: Ages 10-11 © A & C BLACK

Story to script

• Rewrite the passage as a boxed: play script .

Alice had joined a tea party where the March Hare, the Mad Hatter and the Dormouse were sitting around the table.

'Have some wine,' the March Hare said in an encouraging tone.

Alice looked all round the table, but there was nothing on it but tea. 'I don't see any wine,' she remarked.

'There isn't any,' said the March Hare.

'Then it wasn't very civil of you to offer it,' said Alice angrily.

'It wasn't very civil of you to sit down without being invited,' said the March Hare.

'I didn't know it was your table,' said Alice. 'It's laid for a great many more than three.'

'Your hair wants cutting,' said the Hatter. He had been looking at Alice for some time with great curiosity, and this was his first speech.

Alice's Adventures in Wonderland by Lewis Carroll

Script	
Character	**Spoken words (and stage directions)**

NOW TRY THIS!

• Write notes about how the set might look for this scene.

You need not write complete sentences. Use abbreviations.

Teachers' note After the children have read the passage individually, ask them to read it in groups of three, with different children taking the three parts. Discuss which parts of the text are not read, and why, and how these and the spoken words can be shown in a script. You could import a story from the internet and develop a script for it on the interactive whiteboard.

100% New Developing Literacy Sentence Structure and Punctuation: Ages 10-11 © A & C BLACK

Flashback

The │ flashbacks │ **say what had happened before.**

- **Rewrite the flashbacks using the past tense with │ had │ .**

The first one has been completed for you.

1 Jason looked up at the old clock on the tower.

He had seen that clock somewhere before.

> He saw that clock somewhere before.

2 The sound of a piano came through the open window.

_____

_____

> Where has she heard that tune before?

3 There was a shopping centre beside the station.

_____

_____

> Once there was a castle on that very spot.

4 There was something different about the room.

_____

_____

> Someone wound the old clock that has not worked for years.

5 They heard that the house was haunted.

_____

_____

> A young woman died there from a broken heart, it is said.

NOW TRY THIS!

- **Choose a flashback.**
- **Write three sentences about it as if it is happening now.**

Imagine you have gone back in time.

Teachers' note Read the first example with the children and discuss how the past tense changes when it refers to something that happened before the past-tense incident (*Jason looked up at the old clock on the tower*). Focus on the auxiliary verb *had* and remind the children of the purpose of auxiliary verbs in creating tenses.

100% New Developing Literacy
Sentence Structure and
Punctuation: Ages 10-11
© A & C BLACK

Active sentences

This is an | active | verb: broke.

This is an active sentence:

Stella broke the window.

subject   verb   object

The subject of an active verb does the action.

Stella

The object has the action done to it.

The window

• **Complete the sentences with active verbs.**

Subject	Verb	Object
Mr Gray		some toast.
The family		a new television.
Two frogs		flies.
Ella and Sam		the bell.
The engineer		the boiler.
The police officer		a burglar.
The sunshine		the snow.
Mum's hairdresser		a prize.
An old tomcat		a mouse.
The postman		the mail.
Two chefs		a delicious soup.
The children		their lunch.
The musician		the piano.
Alan's sister		her hair.

NOW TRY THIS!

• **Write six sentences that have an | active | verb with no | object |.**

Example: Sheila snored.

Teachers' note Read the example sentence with the children and ask them who did the action, and to what. Remind them that *broke* is an active verb because it says what Stella did. You could ask them to express this sentence in the passive form (*The window was broken by Stella*) and point out the passive verb *was broken*.

100% New Developing Literacy Sentence Structure and Punctuation: Ages 10-11 © A & C BLACK

Passive sentences

This is a | passive | **verb:** was broken.

This is a passive sentence:

<u>The window</u> <u>was broken</u> by <u>Stella</u>.

^ subject   ^ verb   ^ object

The subject of a passive sentence has the action done to it.

The window

• **Complete the sentences with passive verbs.**

Subject	Verb		Object
The bridge		by	heavy traffic.
Their house		by	a local firm.
Many people		by	the bull.
The parcel		by	the post office.
Newcastle United		by	Liverpool.
We		by	a loud crash.
The gang		by	the police.
All the bread		by	mice.
The athletes		by	a sportswear firm.
The racehorse		by	a famous jockey.
The lost dog		by	two boys.
Two of the plays		by	William Shakespeare.
The beautiful lake		by	pollution.

The object does the action.

Stella

NOW TRY THIS!

• **Write six sentences that have a | passive | verb but do not name the object.**

Example: The grass was cut.

Teachers' note Read the example sentence with the children and ask them what had the action done to it, and by whom. Remind them that *was broken* is a passive verb because it says what was broken. You could ask them to express this sentence in the active form (*Stella broke the window*) and point out the active verb *broke*.

100% New Developing Literacy
Sentence Structure and
Punctuation: Ages 10-11
© A & C BLACK

Older English

English is changing all the time:
- new words are made up
- words drop out of use
- grammar changes.

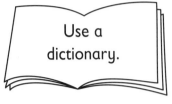

Use a
dictionary.

- **Write these sentences in modern English.**

Pray allow me to
go out to play.

Their house has a parlour, two
bed-chambers, a kitchen and a scullery,
with a courtyard outside.

_____

_____

_____

Would that I had a
new pair of boots.

Thou may'st be fair and beauteous
but thou art wicked. Get thee gone.

_____

_____

_____

Says he so?
I believe him not.

It is cold, is it not? Would it not be best to
remain indoors? What say you to that?

_____

_____

_____

NOW TRY THIS!

- **Look up these older words and write their meanings:**
behold brethren gainsay lo o'er prithee spake yonder
- **Write sentences using the older words.**

Teachers' note The children could collect from parents, grandparents or older teachers
expressions that they used when they were children but which are no longer used or now sound
old-fashioned. Include examples from all the languages spoken in the class. Draw out that
languages are constantly changing and new ways of putting sentences together are developing.

100% New Developing Literacy
Sentence Structure and
Punctuation: Ages 10-11
© A & C BLACK

Standardised

- **Underline the parts of the passage which are not in** standard English .
- **Write them on the four lists to show why they are** non-standard English .

'There's <u>nowt</u> to do here,' said Mina to her mother. 'It's <u>right</u> boring. I knew it would be as soon as <u>I seen</u> the place.'

'Go and ask Sam if he'll learn you to play croquet,' said her mother. 'I thought I seen him in the garden. He can't of gone far.'

Mina found Sam and said to him, 'I wish Mum hadn't of went to that talk about holidays. She wouldn't of brought us here. She thinks it's dead posh but it's just boring. Can you borrow me some money to buy a comic?'

'No – sorry I <u>haven't got none</u> on me. Tell you what – our Rick weren't nowhere to be seen this morning,' said Sam. 'He done the right thing going to town. There isn't nowt to do here.'

Then Mina had an idea: 'Let's get our cozzies and go swimming. It can't never be as bad as staying here being bored out of our skulls.'

Wrong part of verb	Standard word used in a non-standard way	Double negative	Dialect or slang word (and meaning)
I seen	right	haven't got none	nowt (nothing)

NOW TRY THIS!

- **Listen to, or read, another text containing non-standard English.**
- **List the examples of non-standard English.**
- **Explain why these were used.**

Teachers' note Remind the children that standard English uses correct grammar and no dialect words or expressions and can be understood by anyone who speaks English; this is why it should be used for formal writing. Then read the passage aloud. Draw out that many people use non-standard English in conversation, especially when speaking to their families or people they know well.

100% New Developing Literacy
Sentence Structure and
Punctuation: Ages 10-11
© A & C BLACK

All official

- **Cut out the cards and place them face down.**
- **Take turns to pick up a card.**
- **Read it aloud, then say it in** everyday language .

✂

The families and friends of employees of Whiz Co are not eligible for entry in this competition.	For the comfort of other customers, passengers are requested to refrain from putting their feet on the seats.	The use of these appliances is prohibited to persons under the age of 18.
The proprietors reserve the right to refuse admittance to persons they deem unsuitable.	Members are politely requested not to stand beverages or spin coins on the snooker tables.	It is prohibited to deposit waste of any type on this land.
Dogs must be kept under control at all times and owners are required to place dog waste in the bins provided.	This is a pedestrian area. All vehicles are prohibited.	Visitors are requested to proceed with caution. Several headstones in this cemetery are unstable.
Competition winners will be announced in this publication and notified by post.	The use of mobile telephones is prohibited in this area.	Customers are requested to take a ticket and wait for their number to be displayed.

NOW TRY THIS!

- **List the ways in which** official language **is different from everyday language. Think about person, active or passive verbs and vocabulary.**

Teachers' note Explain that official language is used for public notices and for written English addressed to groups, especially for instructions or regulations. Ask the children to comment on features of official language: passive verbs, the third person and formal vocabulary. Discuss why such language is needed: to be clear, polite and authoritative and possibly to avoid legal liability.

100% New Developing Literacy Sentence Structure and Punctuation: Ages 10–11 © A & C BLACK

In official terms

- **Cut out the cards.**
- **Match each** official **word or phrase to an everyday word or phrase.**

Official words and phrases (O)

subject to availability ○	to refrain from ○	imprisonment ○
prohibited ○	currently ○	requested ○
excepting ○	overleaf ○	false declaration ○

Everyday words and phrases (E)

now E	asked E	if we have any E
not to E	going to jail E	not allowed E
on the next page E	lie E	not counting E

NOW TRY THIS!

- **Collect other examples of official language.**
- **Make a glossary of official words and phrases.**

Use a dictionary.

Teachers' note The children may need dictionaries to check the meanings of the more difficult words and phrases in order to match them to the everyday words and phrases. They could also compose sentences using official and then everyday language and describe the context in which each one might be used.

100% New Developing Literacy
Sentence Structure and
Punctuation: Ages 10-11
© A & C BLACK

Impersonally speaking

● **Write the instructions in** ☐ impersonal ☐ **language.**

Children under eleven – bring a grown-up with you.

LIFEGUARD

If you don't live here, don't park your car here.

Under 11s must be accompanied
by an adult.

_____

_____

Passengers – fasten your seatbelt.

If you don't work here, keep out.

_____

_____

Buy yourself a ticket before you get on the train.

Books live on the shelves.

_____

_____

Impersonal word- and phrase-bank

accompanied	except	purchased	requested
adult	employees	readers	required
boarding	no admittance	replace	residents

NOW TRY THIS!

● **Explain how you changed four of the instructions.**
● **Tell a partner.**

Teachers' note Read the first example with the children and ask them if they would expect an official notice to be written in this way, and why not. Draw out that it is informal and might be used on an informal television advertisement addressed to children but not on an official notice, say in a public building.

**100% New Developing Literacy
Sentence Structure and
Punctuation: Ages 10-11
© A & C BLACK**

All in a dialect

- **Read the sentences.**
- **Underline the** dialect **words.**
- **Write their meanings in standard English above the dialect words.**

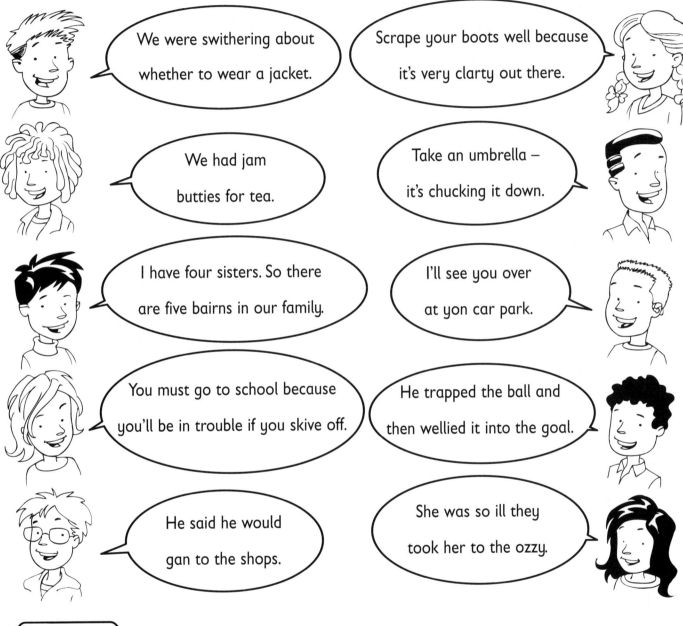

We were swithering about whether to wear a jacket.

Scrape your boots well because it's very clarty out there.

We had jam butties for tea.

Take an umbrella – it's chucking it down.

I have four sisters. So there are five bairns in our family.

I'll see you over at yon car park.

You must go to school because you'll be in trouble if you skive off.

He trapped the ball and then wellied it into the goal.

He said he would gan to the shops.

She was so ill they took her to the ozzy.

NOW TRY THIS!

- **Write any dialect words you know for:**
  - **different foods**
  - **weather**
  - **feelings.**

Teachers' note If possible, address the children in a dialect they do not know. Can they understand what you are saying? Then use a dialect they know. Do they understand this? Explain that dialects are forms of English understood by groups of people, usually from the same region. They should be used only in informal communication because some people may not understand them.

100% New Developing Literacy Sentence Structure and Punctuation: Ages 10-11 © A & C BLACK

Getting technical

- **Underline the** technical **words in the weather report.**
- **Look up their meanings.**
- **Write these in the glossary.**

Use a dictionary.

- **Talk to a partner about what the weather was like.**

Visibility was fairly poor but it improved and high cirrus clouds appeared in the clear sky. The <u>barometer</u> reading began to fall. The wind became squally and southerly. The temperature rose to 15°C but, as cloud cover increased, it fell to 10°C. Clouds thickened and became lower as a layer of nimbostratus formed. The barometer reading continued to fall and precipitation became heavy. A blustery westerly wind was now blowing. The clouds thinned and precipitation grew lighter. The wind became northerly and the barometer reading rose.

Glossary

barometer
_____
_____
_____
_____
_____
_____
_____
_____
_____
_____
_____
_____
_____

NOW TRY THIS!

- **Rewrite the weather report in the simple language of a TV weather report.**

Teachers' note After the children have underlined the technical words, ask them if they know what these words mean. Give the class the opportunity to explain any they know before they look them up. They should write the glossary in alphabetical order. They might need some scrap paper on which to try this out. Some might need help with words that begin with the same letter.

100% New Developing Literacy Sentence Structure and Punctuation: Ages 10-11 © A & C BLACK

Bake a sentence

- **Write long sentences that include the information from each ingredient.**

Use connectives and punctuation to help.

The baby cried.

He was hungry.

His mother fed him.

_____

It was dark.

Tony picked up a torch.

He crept out into the garden.

He was looking for a secret trapdoor.

_____

The old man sat on the bench.

He was reading a newspaper.

He was watching the door opposite.

The door opened slightly.

_____

The old man's head bent over the newspaper.

His eyes were raised.

He watched the door.

A woman stepped out of the door.

_____

NOW TRY THIS!

- **Write four short sentences about a scene in a story.**
- **Join them to make one long sentence.**

Teachers' note Model how to complete the first sentence by thinking aloud: 'The baby cried. Why? Because he was hungry. So his mother fed him.' Then write the sentence *The baby cried because he was hungry, so his mother fed him*. Discuss the changes you made in order to combine the information: the addition of connectives and punctuation.

100% New Developing Literacy
Sentence Structure and
Punctuation: Ages 10-11
© A & C BLACK

I wonder

In these sentences one $\boxed{\text{verb}}$ depends on another.

- **Complete the sentences with** $\boxed{\text{clauses}}$ **that begin with** $\boxed{\text{if}}$ **or** $\boxed{\text{whether}}$.

Mum said I can come to the party _____

_____ .

I am not sure _____ .

They read the book to find out _____ .

No one knows _____ .

The football match will be cancelled _____ .

I am allowed to go to the park _____ .

Dad said he would find out _____ .

_____

we are going to live in Australia.

_____

our town would be a cleaner place to live.

_____

we'll be able to go sledging and build snowmen.

NOW TRY THIS!

- **Write six sentences using** $\boxed{\text{unless}}$.

Teachers' note Explain that these sentences contain something unknown: an *if* or *whether* clause. The children should think up a clause linked to the main clause with *if* or *whether* but it is not necessary to explain this in terms of a subordinate clause. Ask them to add a beginning or an ending which begins *if* or *whether* to complete the sentence so that it makes sense.

100% New Developing Literacy Sentence Structure and Punctuation: Ages 10-11 © A & C BLACK

If...

• **Write these sentences in the** ⟨past tense⟩.

Change the auxiliary verbs to <u>could</u>, <u>should</u> or <u>would</u>.

We can play indoors if it rains.

We could play indoors
_____

_____

My brother will lend me his bike if I ask him.

_____

_____

I cannot paint a picture unless I find a paintbrush.

_____

_____

She does not know whether she can go swimming.

_____

_____

He thinks he will be able to come if his brother is with him.

_____

_____

I do not want to go if I shall be the only one who has to wear a uniform.

I want to know if worms can hear.

_____

_____

NOW TRY THIS!

• **Write six more past tense sentences using**

⟨if⟩, ⟨whether⟩ **or** ⟨unless⟩.

Teachers' note It would be helpful if the children had already completed page 28. Remind them of the *if* and *whether* sentences they wrote and tell them that these are similar but that they should be written in the past tense: for example, *We could play indoors if it rained.* Point out the importance of the auxiliary verbs.

100% New Developing Literacy Sentence Structure and Punctuation: Ages 10-11 © A & C BLACK

Supposing

- **Complete each sentence with a** | clause |.

Use verbs such as <u>could</u>, <u>would</u> or <u>should</u>.

Imagine a city without traffic:
how quiet it would be.

Picture the classroom with
no furniture: _____
_____
_____

Think about learning to dance:
_____
_____
_____

Let's suppose there is life on Mars:
_____
_____
_____
_____
_____

Suppose you were invisible:
_____
_____
_____
_____
_____

Consider a world with no birds:
_____
_____
_____
_____
_____

If only I could have a dog:
_____
_____
_____

I wish I could fly:
_____
_____
_____
_____

NOW TRY THIS!

- **Choose one of the sentences.**
- **Write a paragraph about what** | might | **happen.**

Teachers' note Read the example to the children: cover the subsidiary clause and read only the main clause and discuss how the sentence might be completed before revealing the subsidiary clause. Draw attention to the verb, particularly the auxiliary verb *would* and point out that this expresses something which *might* happen or, in the past, which *might have* happened.

100% New Developing Literacy
Sentence Structure and
Punctuation: Ages 10-11
© A & C BLACK

The sentence improver

- **Read each sentence aloud.**
- **Rewrite it in a better way.**

Example:

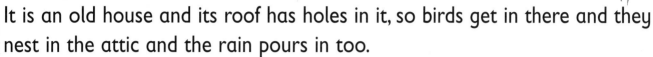
You could take out or add words and use punctuation.

It is an old house and its roof has holes in it, so birds get in there and they nest in the attic and the rain pours in too.

Holes in the roof of the old house let the rain pour in and birds nest in the attic.

Sasha asked Paul and Amrit what kind of sandwiches they like and Paul said ham and Amrit said cheese then Sasha went shopping.

_____

_____

_____

We have never been on holiday and we think this is because Mum cannot afford it but she never says that is why and says that we can find plenty to do close to home and she is right.

_____

_____

_____

We went to the library then we went to the shops and after that we went to Gran's but the first thing we did was to call at Jeff's.

_____

_____

_____

NOW TRY THIS!

- **Make a list of words which help you to write long sentences: for example,** | having |, | when |, | which | **.**

Teachers' note Read aloud the example and ask the children if they can think of anything that is wrong with it. Establish that it reads as if the person who wrote it did not think about the whole sentence before writing it but added to it as he or she went along. This makes it clumsy and it can be improved. Show the improved sentence.

100% New Developing Literacy
Sentence Structure and
Punctuation: Ages 10-11
© A & C BLACK

Invisible nouns

Some nouns are names of feelings, conditions and other ideas.

- **Write a noun for each idea.**
- **Write a sentence for each noun.**

These nouns are not names of objects.

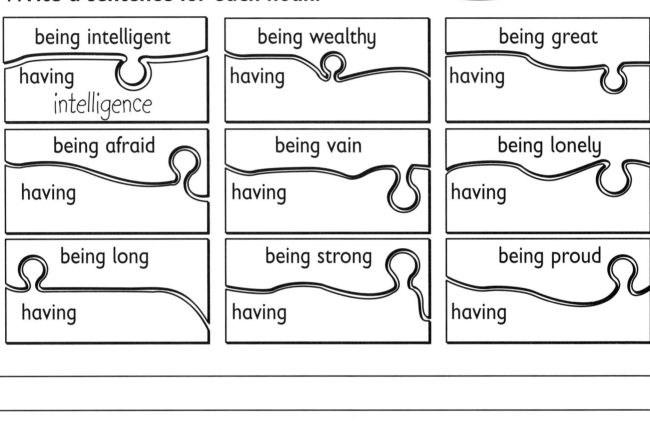

being intelligent	being wealthy	being great
having *intelligence*	having	having
being afraid	being vain	being lonely
having	having	having
being long	being strong	being proud
having	having	having

_____

_____

_____

_____

_____

_____

_____

_____

NOW TRY THIS!

- **Write sentences using six other** abstract nouns .

Teachers' note Explain that this page is about nouns for things which cannot be seen, touched, heard, smelled or tasted. You could introduce the term *abstract noun* if appropriate. Remind the children of their previous year's work on nouns for feelings and read the completed example with them.

100% New Developing Literacy
Sentence Structure and
Punctuation: Ages 10–11
© A & C BLACK

Proverbial prepositions

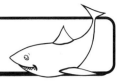

A **preposition** shows how a noun is connected with the rest of the sentence.

- Write a preposition in each gap in the **proverbs**.

Preposition-bank

according to

among   at

before   between

for   from

in   into

on   out of

to   under

with   ~~without~~

There is no smoke _without_ fire.

Charity begins _____ home.

Great oaks grow _____ little acorns.

Always look _____ the bright side.

The streets of London are paved _____ gold.

Time and tide wait _____ no one.

Look _____ you leap.

You can't make a silk purse _____ a sow's ear.

There is nothing new _____ the sun.

There's many a slip _____ cup and lip.

There is no honour _____ thieves.

You can't fit a quart _____ a pint pot.

Cut your coat _____ your cloth.

Don't carry all your eggs _____ one basket.

All roads lead _____ Rome.

NOW TRY THIS!

- **Choose three proverbs of your own.**
- **Underline the prepositions.**

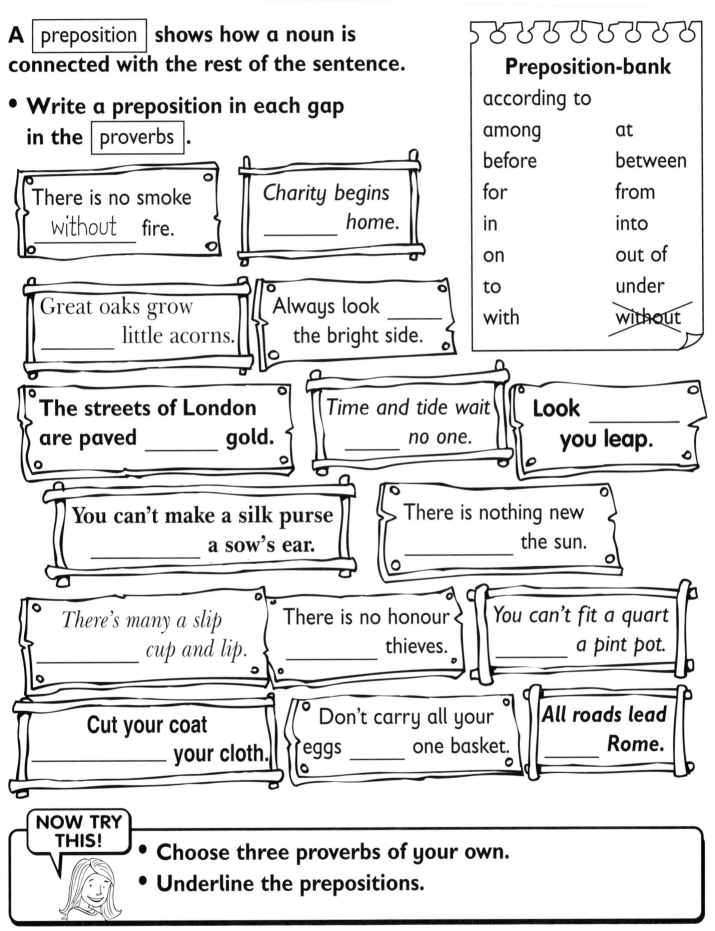

Teachers' note The children should first read some examples of proverbs. This could be linked with work in religious education. Explain that a preposition is a type of connective word and that they are used in many proverbs. During the plenary session ask the children what type of word is linked to the rest of the sentence by the preposition (a noun).

100% New Developing Literacy
Sentence Structure and
Punctuation: Ages 10–11
© A & C BLACK

Adverbial arrows

- **Add an** `adverb` **to each sentence to say more about a verb.**

Use the clue on the target.

- **Rewrite the sentence.**

He lifted the baby out of the cot.

with care

_____

They all lived together in the tiny cottage.

with happiness

_____

She scribbled a note.

without care

_____

The dog eyed the roast beef.

with hunger

_____

I watched a snowflake land on the leaf.

in silence

_____

NOW TRY THIS!

- **Write sentences using adverbs that mean:**

making a noise	being selfish	being generous	with clumsiness	in haste

Teachers' note Remind the children that an adverb or adverb phrase (adverbial) says more about a verb and complete the first example with them. This could be linked with work on suffixes (adding -ly to adjectives to form adverbs) so that the children also learn the associated spelling rules. Discuss the different purposes of adjectives and adverbs.

100% New Developing Literacy Sentence Structure and Punctuation: Ages 10-11 © A & C BLACK

It's imperative

- **Write the instructions using** | imperative verbs |.

You might need to change, add or remove some words.

1
Customers should take a ticket from the machine and wait for their number to show on the screen.

1 Take a ticket
_____
_____
_____

2
Visitors should park in the marked parking bays but not along the roads.

2 _____
_____
_____

3
Drivers should switch off the engine before filling the tank with fuel.

3 _____
_____
_____

4
They should not use mobile phones on the forecourt.

4 _____
_____

5
They should not let children use the fuel pump or air line.

5 _____
_____

6
They should not make unnecessary noise, especially at night.

6 _____
_____
_____

NOW TRY THIS!

- **Write six instructions for visitors to a zoo.**

Use imperative verbs.

Teachers' note Remind the children of their previous learning about writing instructions. What do they know about the way in which the verbs are written in instructions and where the verbs are placed in the sentences? Use the first example to model this.

100% New Developing Literacy
Sentence Structure and
Punctuation: Ages 10-11
© A & C BLACK

Get connected

Connective | words and phrases join parts of sentences in different ways.

• Use connectives to add a clause or phrase to these sentences.

Choose a connective from the group that matches the sentence number.

1a At the new leisure centre there is a gym _and swimming pool._

1b I like the new cafe _____

2a At the seaside you can go surfing _____

2b In the park you can choose _____

3a I am not allowed out this weekend _____

3b Dad sold his old car _____

4a Mum said she will help Mrs Lee _____

4b We are going out walking _____

5a The band kept playing the same tune _____

5b They play that tune _____

6a We ran to the edge of the lawn _____

6b Rats can find food and shelter _____

Connective-bank

1 Adding information
and   but   whereas

2 Adding a choice
either   or   neither   nor

3 Adding reason or purpose
as   because   to
in order to   so   so that

4 Adding a choice or condition
although   even if   except
if   in case   rather than
unless   whether

5 Linking by time
after   as   before   since
until   when   whenever   while

6 Linking by place
where   wherever

Teachers' note Remind the children of what they know about connectives and point out the different purposes they have, as shown on the connective-bank. Point out that different types of word are used as connectives, including prepositions (see page 33).

100% New Developing Literacy
Sentence Structure and
Punctuation: Ages 10–11
© A & C BLACK

Recount connectives

- **Write a sentence about each event.**
- **Use** | time connectives |.

> Show the order in which the events happened.

Walking home from school. Passed shop. Heard alarm and scream.

Hid behind wall. Called 999 on mobile phone.

Van outside shop. Two men in stocking masks came out of shop. Got into van.

10 minutes – police car arrived. Gave police details.

Connective-bank

after	now
as	since
before	until
meanwhile	when
next	while

_____

_____

_____

_____

_____

_____

_____

NOW TRY THIS!

- **Write notes about what happened next.**
- **Use connectives to help you to turn your notes into sentences.**

> Work with a partner.

Teachers' note The children could begin by reading a short recount. Ask them what this type of text is for (to tell the reader about a sequence of events, which could be fiction or non-fiction). Discuss the tense in which it is written and how the connectives link sentences and parts of sentences – usually to show a time connection.

100% New Developing Literacy
Sentence Structure and
Punctuation: Ages 10-11
© A & C BLACK

Argument connectives

- **Use** logical connectives **to link the two points of view in each argument.**

Connective-bank

although	however
because	if
but	since
even if	whereas
on the other hand	

It is cruel to test medicines on animals.

We wouldn't have many of our medicines if they hadn't been tested on animals.

_____

_____

_____

_____

To save energy we should do without street lights.

Some people would be scared to go out.

Homework should be banned. Children need leisure time.

Homework helps them to understand what they learn at school.

_____

_____

_____

Dogs make the park filthy. They should be banned.

Some people have nowhere else to walk their dogs.

_____

_____

_____

_____

_____

_____

NOW TRY THIS!

- **Write two points of view on another argument.**
- **Use logical connectives to link them.**

Teachers' note The children could begin by reading a short argument. Ask them what this type of text is for (to present a viewpoint through argument). Discuss the tense in which it is written and how the connectives link sentences and parts of sentences – usually to show choices or conditions.

100% New Developing Literacy Sentence Structure and Punctuation: Ages 10-11
© A & C BLACK

Remember the colon

- **Put a** colon **in each sentence.**

1 The Kennel Club classifies dogs in six groups hounds, gundogs, terriers, utility, working and toy.

2 Gundogs have been bred to work with shooters one type of gundog, the terrier, is used for chasing rabbits out of their burrows.

3 The working group includes border collies they are excellent herders.

4 Here are some examples of utility dogs poodle, bulldog, chow chow and dalmatian.

5 The labradoodle is a new type of crossbreed it is a labrador crossed with a poodle.

6 There is a famous cartoon beagle he is, of course, Snoopy.

7 A rough collie became the star of many films her name is Lassie.

8 The part of Lassie was played by different dogs some of them were male.

9 There are four things a dog owner should buy a feeding and water bowl, a collar and name tag, a lead and a brush or comb.

- **Read the sentences aloud with a partner.**
- **Check that the colons are correct.**

NOW TRY THIS!

- **Choose five sentences from above.**
- **Rewrite them so that they say the same but do not need colons.**

You might need to change some words.

Teachers' note Begin by reading the first sentence as it is written with no pause where the colon should be (after *groups*). Does it sound right? Discuss what it is about (the groups into which the Kennel Club classifies dogs). Draw out that the first part of the sentence says that the Kennel Club classifies dogs and that the second part names the groups. Ask where the colon should go.

100% New Developing Literacy
Sentence Structure and
Punctuation: Ages 10–11
© A & C BLACK

Remember the semi-colon

In many sentences you can replace a connective with a | semi-colon |. The semi-colon shows that two ideas are connected in some way.

| We went to Spain for our holiday but the Grays went to Italy. | → | We went to Spain for our holiday; the Grays went to Italy. |

• **Rewrite these sentences.**
• **Replace a connective with a semi-colon.**

Like you, I enjoy swimming but, unlike you, I can't dive.	→	
The mist is clearing so we should be able to go to the beach.	→	
We could play cards but on the other hand we could play on the computer.	→	
Ella plays the piano but Toby plays the clarinet.	→	
There is a 'halo' around the moon so it will probably be frosty tomorrow.	→	

NOW TRY THIS!

• **Write three more sentences with two clauses separated by a semi-colon.**
• **Rewrite them with connectives instead of semi-colons.**

Teachers' note Begin by reading the example. Ask the children how the sentence has been changed. Which word has been replaced by a semi-colon? They can then identify the connectives in the other sentences which can be replaced by a semi-colon.

100% New Developing Literacy
Sentence Structure and
Punctuation: Ages 10-11
© A & C BLACK

Commas for separating

- **Read the sentences aloud with a partner.**
- **Put in** | commas | **where they are needed.**

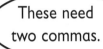
These need one comma.

1   The match starts at half past three not three o'clock.

2   We went to see Buckingham Palace the home of the Queen.

3   Liam chatted non-stop for a long time but Ameen was silent.

4   My brother whispered 'Look at the badgers.'

These need two commas.

5   It was a cold wet windy day.

6   We saw robins starlings wrens and blackbirds.

7   She saw the spider screamed ran away and then felt rather foolish.

8   The children tired after the long walk fell asleep.

9   The pirate ship which had been lurking in the bay finally came ashore.

These need three commas.

10   'Look at the badgers' whispered my brother 'but be very quiet keep still and don't switch on the light.'

11   We need flour eggs milk sugar and butter.

12   He ran up the hill over the bridge through the field past the mill and along the disused railway track.

NOW TRY THIS!

- **Copy four other sentences which have commas.**
- **Read them aloud with and without the commas.**
- **Explain to a partner what difference the commas make.**

Look in fiction or non-fiction texts.

Teachers' note Remind the children that commas can be used for separating parts of a sentence. Read the first sentence as it is written with no pause where the comma should be (after the first *three*). Does it sound right? Which part needs to be separated from the rest? Where should the comma go? Put in the comma where the children suggest, read the sentence again and ask if it sounds right.

100% New Developing Literacy Sentence Structure and Punctuation: Ages 10-11 © A & C BLACK

Commas for clarity

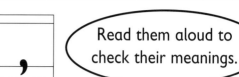

- **Use** commas **to change the meanings of the sentences.**
- **Explain what each sentence means.**

Read them aloud to check their meanings.

The baby I heard weighed nearly four kilograms.	I could hear the baby. It weighed nearly four kilograms.
The baby, I heard, weighed nearly four kilograms.	I heard that
When the light flashed green children crossed the road.	
When the light flashed green children crossed the road.	
He took his dog and a letter which he posted to China.	
He took his dog and a letter which he posted to China.	
She opened her eyes slowly noticing a red stain on the ceiling.	
She opened her eyes slowly noticing a red stain on the ceiling.	
My brother said Ella was wearing a new dress.	
My brother said Ella was wearing a new dress.	

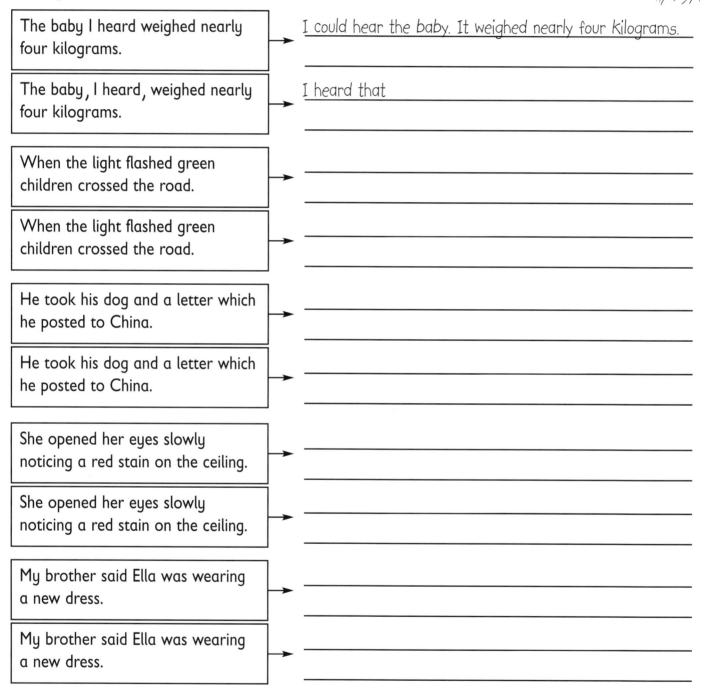

NOW TRY THIS!

- **Copy six sentences from books, signs, leaflets or other texts.**
- **Add or move commas to change the meanings.**

Teachers' note Read the first sentence aloud in a way which suggests the first meaning shown. Then read it again but so that it implies that the speaker did not hear the baby but heard how much it weighed. Ask the children if they think the sentence meant the same thing both times. Invite them to explain the two meanings. What difference did the commas make?

100% New Developing Literacy Sentence Structure and Punctuation: Ages 10-11 © A & C BLACK

Dashes for distance

You can use │ dashes │ to separate a word, phrase or clause from the rest of the sentence:

I can't believe it – a mermaid!

Dashes make stronger breaks than commas. They make a longer pause.

- **Underline the word, phrase or clause to be separated from the rest of the sentence.**
- **Rewrite the sentence using one or two dashes.**

Look a whale!

_____

Hello, it's me Alice.

_____

There was only one thing to do run.

_____

_____

It was Kit and we know what he's like who told me.

_____

_____

Siân lives in that house the one with the red door.

_____

_____

_____

No not chips!

_____

Text me that's if your phone's working tomorrow.

_____

_____

_____

We went with my uncle Raj the one who lives in Manchester to watch Everton.

_____

_____

_____

NOW TRY THIS!

- **Explain why dashes are used here:**
  Chapters 2–3 are about the Second World War
  (1939–1945).

Teachers' note Remind the children that dashes, as well as commas, colons and semi-colons, can be used for separating parts of a sentence. Point out that dashes are used mainly in informal sentences, especially in speech, and that a dash creates a longer pause than a comma. They should read the sentences aloud to decide where to place the dash(es).

100% New Developing Literacy
Sentence Structure and
Punctuation: Ages 10-11
© A & C BLACK

Bracket it

- **Add details to the sentences.**
- **Write them between the** [brackets].

( )

- **Read the sentences aloud.**

She gave £500 to the RSPCA (Royal Society for the Prevention of Cruelty to Animals).

1 He had two dogs (_____) which he walked twice a day.

What type of dogs?

2 Mr Tripp bought a new car (_____) yesterday.

What sort of car?

3 I haven't seen her for ages (_____).

About how long?

4 Please fill in the form (_____) and return it to us.

Say (in one word) that the form is attached.

5 Write a short report (_____) about this issue.

Add that the report should be no more than 250 words.

6 Children (_____) travel at half fare; infants (_____) travel free.

Add that 'children' means those aged from 2 to 15 and that infants are under 2.

7 Our collection is to help the RNIB (_____) and the RNID (_____).

Look up the abbreviations and what they stand for.

NOW TRY THIS!

- **Rewrite the sentences to give the same information but without using brackets. You could use connectives and other punctuation.**

44

Teachers' note Read the example, omitting the parenthesis (the part in brackets). Is it a complete sentence? Now read the entire sentence without pausing for the parenthesis. Does it sound right? The last part was added to explain what RSPCA stands for and it has been surrounded by brackets to help the reader to make sense of the sentence. Finally, read it again, pausing correctly this time.

100% New Developing Literacy Sentence Structure and Punctuation: Ages 10-11
© A & C BLACK

This is your life

- **Decide whether the sentences are from a** ⬚biography⬚ **or an** ⬚autobiography⬚.

- **Write your answers in the boxes.**

> Friends of the family remember the difficult questions he used to ask.

> I longed to go back to the old terrace where I could play all day in the back alley with Jo and Sam.

> My mother slid the three pink teddy bears along the rail of the cot. That is my earliest memory. I was a year old.

> The school was behind our house and I used to squeeze through a gap in the fence to save walking round the block to the children's entrance. That is – until Mr Hoole spotted me.

> Neither Jessica nor her sisters can recall seeing their father without his jacket. They say he disapproved of 'lounging' and expected his children to behave at all times as if they were in the presence of an important guest.

> Mrs Carr owned the sweet shop on the corner, where you could buy four spearmint chews for a penny. We used to call in every day on the way home from school.

> 'I remember the day war broke out,' he told me. 'We were staying with my aunt in Doncaster.' He must have been eleven at the time.

- **Explain how you could tell.**

NOW TRY THIS!

- **Rewrite each passage, changing it from biography to autobiography (or the other way round).**

Teachers' note Explain that a biography is the story of someone's life and ask the children if they know what an autobiography is. Explain that the prefix *auto* means self, so an autobiography is a person's life-story written by him or herself. Tell the children that they should be able to tell which these passages are from the way the writers use language, especially pronouns.

100% New Developing Literacy
Sentence Structure and
Punctuation: Ages 10-11
© A & C BLACK

45

Face the facts

- **Write** | fact | **or** | opinion | **under each sentence.**

Word-bank

I assume	I believe
I expect	I reckon
I suppose	I think

It is likely

It looks as if

It is probable

probably   it seems

Liverpool will win the cup.	Everton have two players injured.

Chelsea have played well all season.	Arsenal have lost six games so far.	The referee knows what he is doing.

The referee gave Crouch a yellow card.	He should have been sent off.

> Think of different ways of writing opinions.

- **Rewrite the opinions so that they do not sound like facts.**

_____

_____

_____

_____

NOW TRY THIS!
- **Listen to a football report.**
- **Write four facts from the report.**
- **Write four opinions.**
- **Rewrite any opinions that sound like facts.**

Teachers' note Revise the meanings of *fact* and *opinion* and point out that some opinions are expressed as if they are facts: for example, *That is brilliant!* Establish that a fact is something which can be measured or checked but an opinion is what someone thinks. Is the first example a fact or an opinion? Ask how it could be expressed to make clear that it is an opinion.

100% New Developing Literacy Sentence Structure and Punctuation: Ages 10-11 © A & C BLACK

Discussion sentences

● **Link the pairs of** opinions **in a sentence.**

A bypass will take traffic away from the High Street.

The village will be safer.

_____

_____

_____

_____

Connective-bank

all the same   also

anyhow   anyway   besides

but   even so   for all that

furthermore   however

in any case   just the same

moreover   nonetheless

nevertheless   too   yet

on the other hand

It will be so much quieter.

It will be noisier for people living near the bypass.

_____

_____

_____

I'm looking forward to being able to walk across the High Street to shop.

The shops might suffer if there are fewer people passing through.

The air will be cleaner and this will improve our health.

The front doors, windows and curtains won't get so dirty.

_____

_____

_____

_____

_____

_____

NOW TRY THIS!

● **Write a discussion using the sentences you wrote.**

Add an introduction and a summary.

Teachers' note Tell the children that each pair of sentences expresses different views or thoughts about the same issue and that their task is to link the two in a sentence which could be part of a discussion: for example, _A bypass will take traffic away from the High Street so the village will be safer._

**100% New Developing Literacy
Sentence Structure and
Punctuation: Ages 10-11**
© A & C BLACK

47

In a leaflet

• **Rewrite these sentences to make Boreville sound more appealing.**

 Add adjectives, adverbs and powerful verbs.

 The thirteenth-century abbey is next to the park.

_____

_____

 The High Street has plenty of shops.

_____

_____

 There are twenty-five restaurants with many types of food: Chinese, Indian, Italian and traditional English.

_____

_____

_____

 Boreville has a very good golf course.

_____

 The leisure centre has an Olympic-sized swimming pool with newly refurbished changing rooms and showers.

_____

_____

_____

NOW TRY THIS!

• **Write five interesting sentences about the place where you live.**
• **Make it sound appealing.**

Teachers' note Invite volunteers to read the sentences aloud. Ask the others if this leaflet sounds interesting and if it makes them want to visit the place. Point out that the same information could be written in a much more appealing way. Remind the children of their previous learning about interesting verbs and adjectives.

100% New Developing Literacy Sentence Structure and Punctuation: Ages 10-11 © A & C BLACK

On the web

This is the home page of a new website for your class.

- Write the headings for the links .

- Write a summary of what is on each link.

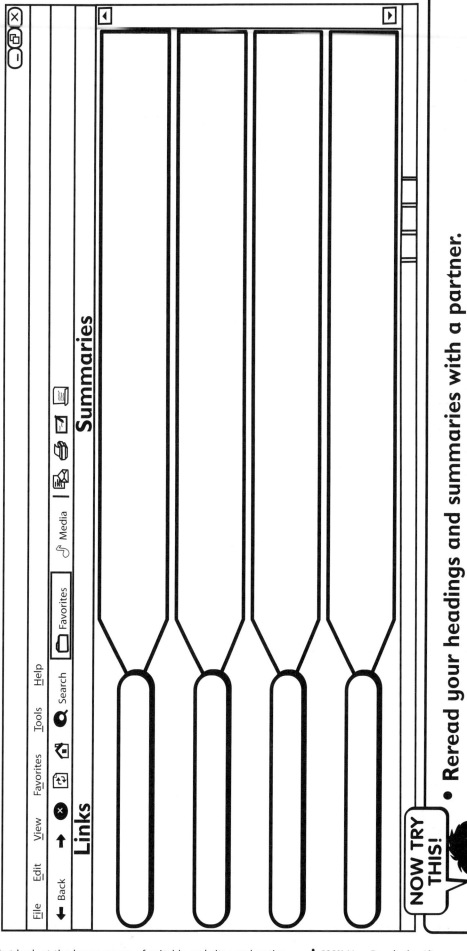

File   Edit   View   Favorites   Tools   Help

← Back   ↑   ✕   🏠   ↻   Search   Favorites   Media

Links

Summaries

NOW TRY THIS!

- Reread your headings and summaries with a partner.
- Improve them with interesting nouns, adjectives, adverbs and verbs.

Teachers' note The children should first look at the home pages of suitable websites and notice how they work, particularly the use of summaries attached to links so that readers know what each link leads to. Emphasise that a summary needs to give the main points or features briefly.

100% New Developing Literacy
Sentence Structure and
Punctuation: Ages 10–11
© A & C BLACK

Notes to script

- Use the notes to help you to write sentences for a television news report.

Notes

Standing on unspoilt beach at Saltsea. Plans to build hotel close to beach.

Peter Hill (developer) – good for local economy. Jobs on building site + in hotel. More tourists → profits for local businesses.

Sam Jones (local farmer) – spoil lovely coast. Damage farm land. Bring pollution. Peace lost. Noise. Council to meet to discuss. Locals bringing petition against hotel.

News report

Think about punctuation.

 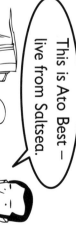

This is Ato Best – live from Saltsea.

_____

_____

_____

_____

_____

_____

_____

_____

_____

_____

_____

_____

_____

NOW TRY THIS!

- Underline the verbs. Which tenses did you use?
- Explain any changes of tense.

Teachers' note Explain that this activity is about a script for a television news report of an issue, presented by someone on the spot. Note that this will be mainly in the present tense because it is about what is going on *now*, but that there should be some past tense verbs (to say what has already happened) and some future tense verbs to say what might happen and what is planned.

100% New Developing Literacy
Sentence Structure and
Punctuation: Ages 10-11
© A & C BLACK

Eyewitness

- **Write a radio news report as if you are watching this scene happening.**

Make it sound exciting.

Good morning. This is _____

_____

_____

_____

_____

_____

_____

_____

_____

Say who and where you are.

Say briefly what has happened.

Say what is happening now.

NOW TRY THIS!

- **Which tenses did you use in the report?**
- **Explain why you used these tenses.**

Teachers' note Explain that this is about a script for a radio news report on an event, presented by someone on the spot. Note that this will be partly in the present tense, about what is going on now, but that some of it will be in the past tense, to say what happened. How will the report differ from a TV report? (The audience cannot see the scene so the reporter has to describe it.)

100% New Developing Literacy
Sentence Structure and
Punctuation: Ages 10-11
© A & C BLACK

Obituary

- **Use the notes to help you to write sentences for an** obituary **about Queen Victoria, dated 7 January, 1901.**

An obituary is about someone who has just died.

Think about tenses and words for time.

Died Tues 6 Jan 1901 after short illness.

Last weeks of life spent at Osborne House on Isle of Wight.

Daughter of Edward, Duke of Kent + Princess Victoria of Saxe-Coburg. Born 24 May 1819.

Became Queen 20 June 1837 when uncle William IV died with no children to succeed him.

Married Prince Albert of Saxe-Coburg 10 Feb 1840.

Use the present tense.

NOW TRY THIS!

- **Find out about Queen Victoria's children and who became king when she died.**
- **Write a sentence about them to end the obituary.**

Teachers' note Provide an obituary for each group to read and then ask them when and why obituaries are written. What are they for? Tell them that they are going to write an obituary about Queen Victoria, based on some notes. Discuss how this will differ from a biography (it will be much shorter and written as if she has just died).

100% New Developing Literacy
Sentence Structure and
Punctuation: Ages 10-11
© A & C BLACK

Hitting the headlines

- **Explain the** | play on words | **in these headlines.**

HOLE IN ROAD COUNCIL LOOKING INTO IT

_____

_____

_____

_____

_____

HOSPITAL SUED BY TEN FOOT DOCTORS

Man shot by shops

_____

_____

_____

_____

_____

DOG MESS ANGERS RESIDENTS – POLICE STEP IN

Children make healthy snacks

_____

_____

_____

_____

_____

Dairy farmers turning to beef

GIANT WAVES DOWN SHIP'S FUNNEL

_____

_____

_____

NOW TRY THIS!

- **Investigate other headlines.**
- **Look for:**

  | puns | ambiguity | homonyms | homophones |

Teachers' note Read the first headline to the children and ask them what picture it conjures up in their minds (council officials looking into a hole). Discuss what else _looking into it_ could mean (investigating what happened). Explain that this is a play on words and ask them to look for the play on words in the other headlines.

100% New Developing Literacy
Sentence Structure and
Punctuation: Ages 10-11
© A & C BLACK

- **Underline sentences that**
  - state facts (green)
  - give opinions (red)
  - persuade (blue).

Work with a partner.

PLASTIC BOTTLES ONLY

COMPOST

We must act now to save the planet.

Everyone can take small actions that will have a big effect. Yet many people regularly waste energy and fail to recycle their rubbish.

SAVE THE PLANET

Just think – you can help to cut down on carbon dioxide in the atmosphere by cutting down on the amounts of electricity, gas and oil you use. Moreover you will save money at the same time. Just think – you could bring that dream holiday or new computer nearer each time you switch off a device left on standby.

You must realise that rubbish that is not recycled is buried, creating methane gas, or burned, creating carbon dioxide. Not only do these gases pollute the air and contribute to global warming, but also these methods create eyesores which blight the lives of local people. What's more, scientists have confirmed that global warming is causing sea levels to rise.

RECYCLE NOW

Do you want to be responsible for this? Surely not. Act now.

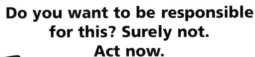

NOW TRY THIS!

- **List the characteristics of persuasive texts.**

Think about types of sentence, tense, verb forms, person and connectives.

Teachers' note Ask the children to read the passage and to notice how it differs from a report. Draw out that a report presents the facts but that this also gives opinions and tries to persuade the reader to share those opinions and to take the suggested actions. Ask the children how it does this: draw attention to persuasive words and phrases, such as *we must*, *yet*, *just think*.

100% New Developing Literacy Sentence Structure and Punctuation: Ages 10-11 © A & C BLACK

Argument sentences

How might you support these statements in an |argument|?

Use connectives or punctuation, or both, to help you to add to the sentence.

- **Add an** |explanation| **or evidence to the sentence.**

We should be allowed to bring our pets to school

_____

_____

Pets should not be allowed into school

_____

_____

Connective-bank

as	because	due to
for	in case	
in order to		lest
on account of		
otherwise		since
so	so that	to

I believe in magic _____

_____

I do not believe in magic _____

_____

There must be life on other planets _____

_____

There could not be life on other planets _____

_____

Table manners are important _____

_____

Table manners are not important _____

_____

NOW TRY THIS!

- **Write three sentences to argue about an issue that is important to you.**

Teachers' note Read the first sentence to the children and ask them if it states a fact or an opinion. Tell them that all the sentences on this page state opinions and that their task is to use a connective to add an explanation or evidence to persuade other people that the opinion is right.

100% New Developing Literacy
Sentence Structure and
Punctuation: Ages 10-11
© A & C BLACK

A strange image

- **Rewrite the sentences about the wood.**
- **Make the wood seem mysterious.**

Add adjectives, adverbs, similes, comparisons, and metaphors

I see trees.

_____

Their branches spread.

_____

_____

Leaves flutter.

_____

_____

Some leaves fall.

_____

_____

Twigs crack under my feet.

_____

_____

I see rough bark.

_____

NOW TRY THIS!

- **Reread your sentences.**
- **Make them into a poem.**
  They need not be sentences in a poem.

Work with a partner.

Teachers' note Tell the children that they are going to read some sentences about an ordinary wood and then change them so that the wood seems mysterious. Discuss the types of words and phrases they could add: such as _like giants, gnarled, like great claws, eerily, like dry bones._

100% New Developing Literacy
Sentence Structure and
Punctuation: Ages 10-11
© A & C BLACK

What a surprise!

- **Add a surprise ending to each sentence.**

Examples:

She opened the fridge _and out flew a parrot._

The gravel path led across the lawn, through the scented blossom of the shrubbery _and into the scrapyard._

We watched the team training: heading, dribbling _____ _____

It was a long, sweeping, sandy beach with sand dunes _____ _____

The baker made bread, cakes, biscuits _____ _____

He sat down at the kitchen table _____ _____

She chose some flowers for her mother: lilies, _____ _____

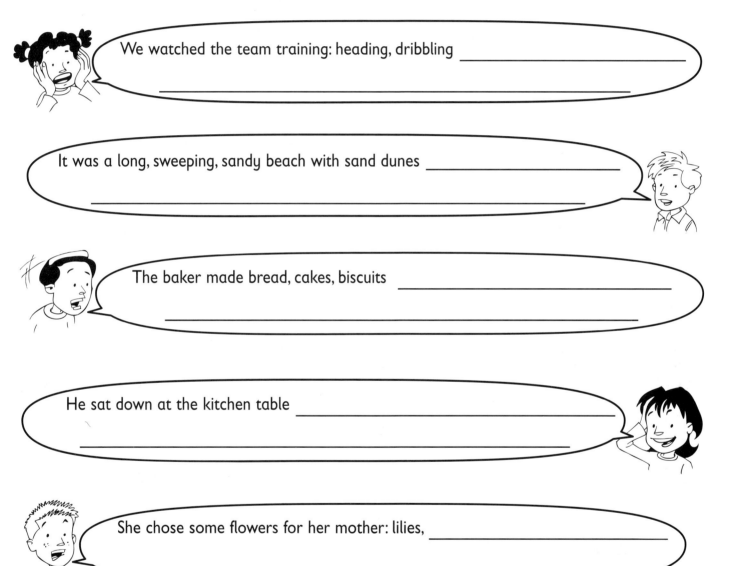

NOW TRY THIS!

- **Use one of the sentences to help you to write a poem in which there is a surprise.**

Your poem need not rhyme.

Teachers' note Read the first completed example to the children, stopping after the first clause. What might happen next? Read the second clause and note that it is not what was expected. Repeat this with the second example. Point out that the children should think about how to link the ending to the rest of the sentence: using punctuation or a connective word or phrase.

100% New Developing Literacy
Sentence Structure and
Punctuation: Ages 10-11
© A & C BLACK

Word play

In these sentences the Mock Turtle plays with the words for school subjects when he talks to Alice.

'Reeling and Writhing, of course, to begin with,' the Mock Turtle replied; 'and then the different branches of Arithmetic – Ambition, Distraction, Uglification, and Derision.'
...

'Well, there was Mystery,' the Mock Turtle replied, counting off the subjects on his flappers, 'Mystery, ancient and modern, with Seaography: then Drawling – the Drawling-master was an old conger-eel, that used to come once a week: he taught us Drawling, Stretching, and Fainting in Coils.'

Alice's Adventures in Wonderland by Lewis Carroll

• **Write the real names of the subjects.**

Reeling	_____	Writhing	_____
Uglification	_____	Ambition	_____
Distraction	_____	Derision	_____
Mystery	_____	Seaography	_____
Drawling	_____	Stretching	_____
Fainting	_____		

• **Make up some funny words the Mock Turtle might use for cooking.**

baking	*faking*	boiling	_____
grilling	_____	roasting	_____
stirring	_____	rolling	_____
chopping	_____	mixing	_____
simmering	_____	icing	_____
freezing	_____	microwaving	_____
peeling	_____	weighing	_____

NOW TRY THIS!

• **Write a conversation between the Mock Turtle and Alice about cooking.**

Alice's Adventures in Sunderland

Teachers' note Read the passages and ask the children if they spotted any play on words. Some children could create similar dialogues to this with a partner or in a group of three or four, trying out ideas before writing them down. Themes they could base these on include names of famous people or teachers or places in the local area.

100% New Developing Literacy
Sentence Structure and
Punctuation: Ages 10-11
© A & C BLACK

The issue

These extracts are from poems about three different issues:

> **1** In fifty-three the children up our road
>   Got television and disappeared indoors
>   After school, instead of coming out
>
> From *Cool Medium* by David Sutton

> **2** Let's say goodbye to hedges
>   And roads with grassy edges
>   And winding country lanes;
>   Let all things travel faster
>   Where motor-car is master
>   Till only Speed remains.
>
> From *Inexpensive Progress* by
> John Betjeman

> **3** Build your houses, build your houses, build your towns,
>   Fell the woodland, to a gutter turn the brook,
>   Pave the meadows, pave the meadows, pave the downs
>
> From *Beleaguered Cities* by F. L. Lucas

What issue is each poet writing about?
What is the poet saying about the issue?
How does the poet use comparisons?

Write your answers on the chart.

Poem	Issue	What the poet says	Comparisons
1	Television	Stops children from playing outdoors	
2			
3			

- **Choose one of these starters and write a short poem of your own about text messages.**

In two thousand all the class…

Let's say goodbye to talking…

Press the keys, press the keys, press the buttons…

Think about how texting affects people's lives.

NOW TRY THIS!

- **Choose another starter from above to write a different poem about texting.**

Teachers' note Ask the children to identify the issue each poet is writing about. They could work in groups to discuss what the poets are saying about these issues and then work together to say how they use comparisons to help. The children should then create their own poem on the issue of text messaging using one of the starters provided.

100% New Developing Literacy
Sentence Structure and
Punctuation: Ages 10-11
© A & C BLACK

In a word

What types of word are <u>underlined</u>?

You can tell from the rest of the sentence.

What a <u>supercalifragilisticexpialidocious</u> day!

Hm… She's describing something. It must be an adjective.

- **Write in the boxes:**

| noun | verb | adjective | adverb |

1 I'd like fish without any <u>accoutrements</u>, please.

2 She had a very <u>capacious</u> bag.

3 He slipped into the house <u>covertly</u>.

4 The play <u>culminated</u> in a lively dance.

5 We saw a picture of a Greek woman wearing a <u>diploidion</u>.

6 They <u>ensconced</u> themselves behind the curtains.

7 She spoke <u>eloquently</u> about the journey.

8 There was a scent of <u>frangipani</u> in the garden.

9 The sudden chill made her arms become <u>horripilated</u>.

10 The elephant lurched <u>ponderously</u> across the plain.

NOW TRY THIS!

- **Find six difficult words.**
- **Look up their meanings.**
- **Write each word in a sentence.**
- **Ask a partner what types of word they are.**

Use a dictionary.

Teachers' note Tell the children that they are going to read sentences which contain a word they might not know. Encourage them to use the strategies they have learned to read these words: splitting them into syllables, using phonics, analogy with other words. Even if they do not know what the word means they should be able to deduce from the rest of the sentence what type it is.

100% New Developing Literacy
Sentence Structure and
Punctuation: Ages 10-11
© A & C BLACK

Punctuation check

- **Add punctuation to the passage to make the meaning of each sentence clear.**

The Old Woman who Lived in a Posh Training Shoe (left foot)

My council tax said the woman is far too high If I lived in a high-heeled shoe it would be a different matter but this shoe is low so my council tax should be low

The council official lay flat on the ground to speak to her since she was only 6cm tall His feet rested in the garden of number 64 at the other end of the street He couldn't see what the householders children were doing to his shoes selling them as very posh homes in all probability

Madam the council official replied tax is not based on height but on the value of your property This is a very desirable expensive training shoe at the upper end of the market

It is less than a thousandth of the size of a normal house and so the tax should be a thousandth of the normal tax she said Whats more this left shoe has no value whatsoever without the right shoe

Meanwhile he could hear the construction workers making a start on his very stylish right shoe Four bedrooms at least said one And an ensuite bathroom in the toe area added another not to mention the walk in wardrobe

He shifted his foot slightly Theres some movement in this property he heard Well have to treat that first Yes an axe will be very useful

He shook his feet vigorously upon which a clamour of voices demanded compensation forms Our shoe has been kicked into Sole Street said one Thats a right slum

Look at our eyelets said another Id just made new curtains for them and Id just swept the tongue and laces Hes got a lot to answer for Theyve got to stop sending giants out here

Mm said another but their shoes come in handy

NOW TRY THIS!

- **Write six sentences to add to the story.**
- **Check your punctuation.**

Teachers' note Tell the children that the passage they are going to read has no punctuation marks apart from the brackets in the title and a hyphen. They should read it silently and decide first of all where each sentence ends. They can then add full stops, question marks and exclamation marks, but they should also look out for dialogue. They can then add punctuation within the sentences.

100% New Developing Literacy
Sentence Structure and
Punctuation: Ages 10-11
© A & C BLACK

61

Futuristic

- **Write the verbs in the** | future | **tense.**
- **Use auxiliary verbs:** | shall | | will | | going to |

You (to take) _____ a lot of tests at school very soon,
but before that you (to do) _____ a lot of revision.
I predict that the subjects (to be) _____ English, Maths
and Science. Others in your class also (to take) _____
the same tests. Come back in July and I (to tell) _____
you your results. I foresee that then you (to have)
_____ a long holiday from school and that in September
you (to start) _____ at a new school. You (to learn)
_____ some new subjects. Now you (to pay)
_____ me five pounds, please.

Know Your Future Today

She's right. I (to do)

_____ revision

and tests. I wonder where I

(to go) _____

for my holiday and what else I

(to do) _____

in the summer.

NOW TRY THIS!

- **Write six sentences about events you know are going to take place.**

Teachers' note Tell the children that the verbs have been taken out of this passage but that there is a clue for each one. They should look at the clue and write the future tense of the verb to match the person: they can check this by noticing the pronouns: *I, you* and so on.

100% New Developing Literacy
Sentence Structure and
Punctuation: Ages 10-11
© A & C BLACK

Past problem

- **Rewrite the passage in the past tense.**
- **Use different forms of the past tense, for example:**

| went | was going | has gone | had gone | could have gone |

| would have gone | should have gone | had been going |

After two minutes Carrick shoots, but it goes straight to Casillas, who punches it out – straight to Dyer. Surely he should score – but, no, the flag goes up for off side. Now Gerrard has the ball but he loses it in a tackle.

Spain are beginning to attack. Villa has a chance. It should go in, but he misses. Now after sixteen minutes Villa flicks the ball to Morientes. He can't miss – but the ball goes over the bar. Neville floats a high cross over to Crouch, who should reach it, but he fails to connect… England have to do better than this if they are going to win the match.

_____

_____

_____

_____

_____

_____

_____

_____

_____

NOW TRY THIS!

- **For a sports report, write six sentences about any sporting event you have watched.**
- **Change these sentences to write a commentary.**

Teachers' note Tell the children that the passage has been written as if the commentator is at the football match, as in a television or radio commentary. Their task is to change it so that it reads more like a newspaper report published after the match.

100% New Developing Literacy
Sentence Structure and
Punctuation: Ages 10-11
© A & C BLACK

Sentence-builder

- Write sentences which contain all the information in the bubbles.

 You might need to change, add or remove words.

 Pia Lee James

James wanted to go to town with Lee.

He didn't think his mother would let him.

He told her he was going to Lee's house.

His mother phoned Lee's mother.

_____

_____

James's mother was very worried.

She heard that he was not at Lee's house.

Lee's mother was worried.

She thought Lee was at James's house.

_____

_____

Pia is Lee's sister.

She heard her mother talking to James's mum.

She sent a text to Lee.

She told him to come home.

_____

_____

Lee showed James the text.

He said, 'We're in trouble.'

He said, 'We'd better go home.'

They set off home.

_____

_____

NOW TRY THIS!

What do you think happened next?
- **Write notes in 'bubbles'.**
- **Use them to write a long sentence.**

Teachers' note Ask the children to read all four sentences in each set and then to think about how to combine all these details in one sentence. Remind them to use punctuation and connectives and point out that they can change the order of the information and take out some words, change some and add others, if necessary.

100% New Developing Literacy
Sentence Structure and
Punctuation: Ages 10-11
© A & C BLACK